Fell Hunger

JOSEPH LENNON

salmonpoetry

Published in 2011 by
Salmon Poetry
Cliffs of Moher, County Clare, Ireland
Website: www.salmonpoetry.com
Email: info@salmonpoetry.com

ISBN 978-1-907056-61-1

COVER IMAGE: From an oil-on-canvas (cm 69.5 x 58.5), ex voto painting attributed to Giovanni Antonio Vanoni (1810-1886), owned by the parish of San Fedele a Verscio in Canton Ticino, Switzerland. Photo credit and thanks to Don Czeslaw Sutor and Mario Manfrina. Thanks also to Museo Regionale Centovalli e Pedemonte, Switzerland.
COVER DESIGN: Siobhán Hutson
AUTHOR PHOTO CREDIT: Doug Keith

Salmon Poetry receives financial support from The Arts Council

For Marika

Acknowledgements

Acknowledgements are due to the editors of the following publications in which some of the poems in this collection previously appeared:

"Hitching Tuam Road" (*Denver Quarterly*, Spring 1999); "Moose," (*The Recorder*, Fall 2000); "29th Birthday," and "If Vermeer Were Here" (*Foilsiú*, Spring 2004); "Melody Lane" (*Natural Bridge*, Spring 2005); "29th Birthday: Skitching" (*Book of Irish-American Poetry from the Eighteenth Century to the Present*, Notre Dame UP, 2007). "1981"; "Making Change"; "Wood Bullet"; "Still Life with Apple"; "If Vermeer were Here"; "Family Country"; "Harmonica Lesson II"; "Sleeping Place (Coemeterium)" (*New Hibernia Review*, Fall 2007); "Harmonica Lesson" (*Poetry Ireland Review*, Spring 2007); "Harmony Lessons" (*From the Small Back Room, A Festschrift for Ciaran Carson*, Netherlea, 2008). Thanks to Jessie Lendennie, Siobhán Hutson, Giancarlo Beneventi, Ronan Kelly, Tyler MacDaniel, Yvonne Murphy, Todd Hearon, Colum McCann, Daniel Collins, June Dwyer, Robin Metz, Daniel Tobin, Margaret Gibson, my parents, J. Michael Lennon and Donna Pedro Lennon, and my wife Marika Beneventi.

Contents

Home Away

Coda

Per Grazia Ricevuta

Crosshatching

Lying in the back of the station
wagon, we stared at the sound-
proofing holes gridding the ceiling;
they'd draw up close or lance out
as our eyes changed focuses.

A diorama of boys, we watched,
through smears of finger-print caucuses
over new fields, lines of trees shrinking east.
We waved at truckers trailing, passing us,
brooding over the great prairie, over
what was close or near no longer,
the familiar, now distant, the wan

open sky above, behind, before us—
the roof whole, then porous.

Home Sick

Self Portrait of the Hunger Artist as a Boy

On the linoleum, holding my belly,
I roll and enfold my thin self.
My parents nudge me out the pantry.
"C'mon now, stop the drama, Joseph.

We'll call you when supper's ready."
I rise and follow the sunset's glow
down the hallway, stepping unsteady,
as tall giraffes upend and buffalo

roam inside the knotted wallboard.
I hunker beneath the front stairs,
my body lean like a twisted chord,
studying Jesus's second-station airs.

A hero of hunger under cracking plaster,
anaemic, wildish after the master.

Still Life with Apple (Complex)

She kept private her canvases and paints,
four frames, deep in the dining-room closet;
they leaned beside the blackthorn canes,
below the wedding cake, off limits by fiat.

A boy in the quiet, I'd slide clear a rectangle
lay it on the rug where it didn't belong
and stare and wonder how a cherry-red apple
could marvel my mother so long.

Brass tacks pulled the thick canvas taut;
it felt like my dad's duffle bag and twine,
or a briny boat cover looped with sailor knots,
oily colour with the tang of turpentine.

I couldn't gaze long so my circling finger traced
that red fruit, outlining what I could not taste.

Melody Lane

was where the cops parked, around the corner from us,
the first turn after the speed zone dropped to village limits.
I still go back to 341 West Main Street, half proud and half not
that our old address could be anywhere in the US of A.

But Chicken Bristle Road could only be near the 4-mile square,
near Possom Trot, down Dannenberger, off Ramsey Road
across the Sangamon River from Honeywell. Back there kids
shot straddling dirt bikes, skinned rabbits, spat with authority.

We grew zucchini for roadside sale, the old Conestoga trail,
mowed lawns, read books, played ball, hopped freight trains.
On Rt. 4 to Staunton, Illinois, Jesus said be ready for his return,
the preacher implored over the radio in mid-western earnest:

> *Turn to the Heart of Jesus. Enter the Burning Furnace of Love;*
> *the Kingdom is close; one day He'll drop from Heaven above.*

But we were Catholic—my dad turned the dial.
Even then I knew no one visited places like this.

Gerald Roof

smiled irony and revolt, smoked, combed back
the coolest 70s feather-cut. Held back to my grade
(and his brother Ronnie's), he didn't give a crap.

Once we sat waiting in the long, narrow hallway—
waxed, Christian. He knew worse than stern looks,
striped ties, black-rimmed glasses. They made me

watch as Principal Gladstone paddled him; he took
it with bravado like a goldfish gulped. I was let off,

lessoned. On breaks from in-school suspension, he'd say
between smokes: "Fuck those jackoffs that ride you."
I tried to tell Ron this at his funeral—we just man-
hugged by the closed casket. Gerald died speeding

from cops, riding wheelies at the lake, blowing chances
on a bike with no plates, freely, under low branches.

Uncle

I refused to say it when Nev Rankin had me in a headlock.
Somehow my skinny body raged blue, tripped his blond mass
onto uneven stone. My grass-stained elbow split his lip,
broke skin, bled as his head conked down. I rammed

his face, electric, a shotgun to boyhood. For all the town
his jaw blood seeped into damp ground. Soon kids hung
over him (not me), helped him comb grass for his tooth.
By the wall I stood in sun, shadow, sun as clouds inhaled
light. My shoulder blades on cold brick, my elbow clotting,
I held my guts. A grain truck rattled on the road, its load
dropped at the elevator. Beaded dust clung to its sides;
its wake stirred cow dung latent in the air.
Neville held his jagged tooth, pinching it,
when we shook hands, a newly cut key.

1981

The Coana brothers spray-painted
the letters, ten-feet high, outside
the gymnasium walls: I R A.
Black letters under a spring sky,
for strikers starving a world away. This'll
solve nothing, my father said as Sands
and the nine flickered on the news.

In the morning, Dean Hochtstader manhand-
led my brother, then me, into his office,
thinking us Irish east-coasters,
the vandals. I swallowed spit,
listened to his heartland politics,
and just barely hid my anger,
so, sure, I fell for hunger.

Aisles

for my brother Jim

In those green aisles that rise and narrow
to a distant pitch, running seems running
in place. You lose perspective as summer
leaves slice you, sharp as gills, long papery
edges cut your arms with strokes as fine as
fishing lines. You shield your face from rows
that swell like green waves. Running in corn
is like running in circles—panic stalks aisles
in fields like bad hunting dogs snap at kids,
like breakers smack bows, like nude limbs
dangle in ocean water. You break away
to the black river, to the railway bridge,
happy to walk the straight miles blind,
knowing trains no longer use the line.

Sleeping Place (Coemeterium)

Every dawn Mr. Beck dragged
his dead leg to the graveyard,
to open the gates and raise the flag.

On my route before breakfast, I'd wave
hard as he squinted for roadkills,
or slid them to the drainage ditch.

Another old man mowed the hills,
rounding in crisp livery. As corpses
rose in grass and blossoms,

they worked the yard with care,
righted tombstones, buried opossums,
straightened wreaths, full and spare.

Always to me their nods simply said:
do not long for an unmade bed.

Host

Taught my dull ache was anxiety—
the ciborium in the hands of the celebrant
might absolve guilt, make me worthy
to receive; I'd pray to see what meant

"Only say the word, and I shall be healed."
Silence at St. Jude's, fasting to communion,
then, my tongue served, I would sit sealed
before ghostly pangs beat my duodenum.

Head down, the mystery, bread to body,
lit like words aflame, like a cross pressed in
to flesh as years of wafers from the ambry
scored jejunum, ileum, combed intestine,

but never became flesh, never my God—
those flights of swallows through my gut.

Solstice

I noticed the year's chill was fading
as the moon hung half-witted on the tree line,
and streetlights stood stranded in welling shade
while moralities dangled from dinner tines.

Out back where fireflies spasmed the dark,
I stepped on tussocks, unshorn, unmastered,
as insects flitted, shone yellow-green sparks:
every light was a call; every call, an answer.

Mystery cannot abide a small town's might,
but strangers can cross circles in a back acre—
where I imagined an intelligence in light:
flashes unite and part, syncing inner aches;

in the moon's long bounce of sun fire,
lit bellies meant hunger, meant desire.

Ten Thousand (Lobsters) Saw I

that summer as they flapped their tails
one by one, fluttering prone on their backs.
I held them down, laid my blade like a sail
along the red seam in the ventral crack,

pressed clean through meat, pointed the knife
to the backs of their bodies, levered the length
of thorax with steel. Opaque gelatinous life
slumped into blue exoskeletons.

Their black eye stalks tossed as I scooped inward,
cracked claws, slit tails, and forked to the grill
bodies turning to meat, red hooks, searing curd.
I plucked their ochre hearts, pumping still,

freed from bodies that swam backward,
nestled beneath crags, claws outward.

(Newport, Rhode Island)

A Matching Outfit for My Birthday

I won't wash clothes today, my twenty-eighth birthday.
The tree men across the road finally finished cutting
the dead branches away. On hearing the racket
I went to the window with my sprawling plants, saw
sagging limbs dropping from trunks. At the bus stop
a woman stood reading a thin book with the aplomb
of a minister spreading fingers over gospel—dressed
in tan shoes, black pants, tan top, black hair around
her tanned face, neck. As she bent to her black bag,
her browned arms blended with her blouse; erased
her clothes, her spine rolled down her naked back.
I hopped down flights to see her read white pages
through black glasses, astounded by the spare
silver running all throughout her hair.

(Boston 1996)

Wood Bullet

for my father and his

Splitting old wood, I found a bullet
sunk 36 rings in a log, a foreign object
grown over like an undigested comment.
Decades ago it seared through thin bark
into a live oak growing. New wood filled
its grooves, and the sapling recovered by
absorbing it, embodying it. Burns smear
the flattened nose where it burst into
the tree, cauterizing the wound it cut.
A half-buried beetle in a log. I thumbed
it out as a secret, as a son reads letters
of his dead father. From that smooth
furrow, it dropped into my palm,
its lead heavier than stone.

(Storrs, Connecticut)

Galesburg Imperium

for Robin Metz

I.

The sisters stood on their porch
trimming nails with shearing scissors.
Up in my window I watched Pearl's
skull, aqua-netted with red wisps,

tuck her sister's arm under her own
and ply her fingers like a child's.
Ruth grimaced, staring beyond
the mass of maples, not yet blind.

Five finished, Pearl lifted by the tips
Ruth's other hand, scrolled open
her fingers, flicked crescent clips
with the blades over the ledge.

After their paring ended,
she sat, stayed, winded.

II.

When town boomed their uncle ran shifts
at the brick factory; their father threw switches
in the changing yards for continental cargoes
going down the B & O or the Rock Island line,

changing at the Quincy Y. That nexus gave way
to trucking; we live in the old interstices
of farmlands, shrinking towns, closing factories,
abandoned jazz joints made on stopovers.

Not only ghosts of Swedish utopians,
Sandburg pilgrims, and college kids cover
town like the Burlington bricks that pock
the forest floor by overrun furnaces.

Wheeling the barrels out, Pearl says:
"I see lights; you're still here."

III.

The pavement like foil flashes as they walk
under thunder in the amber middle of their home.
Pearl passes Ruth's suds-daubed elbows,
slips a plate, a pickle dish, a metal percolator

into the waters. Their company has parted.
Pearl mines silver from the rinse, places forks,
spoons on cotton train towels. Ruth pats
every piece, her cloudy eyes rolling.

Panes rattle down the street,
announcing a thousand-mile wind;
my chimes smash suddenly
as a locomotive hits

Galesburg hunkering, howling,
as the sisters shelve china.

(Galesburg, Illinois)

Fast

On the third day, I felt light. Yes,
not merely less heavy, but in touch—
it came through me. I ached less,
surprised by water, its welcome taste.

Wheat raised ridges inside like razor
lines—without it my flesh rose, tingled,
cool as mists of barnyard sprays (or
dizzy falls on the slick of a shingle)
dousing hay, weighing down chaff.

I felt stronger, weaker, without,
not knowing poison grew like grass,
belly-aches shone a route to truth.
On a threshing floor out of season,
I starved myself for a reason.

Elegy

Darting from a horse's skull,
eddying into sky, a butterfly, up
into burning youth and health,
has fallen with its wings

curled, desiccating. To a
whisper now, my thyroid
beaded with nodules,
goes quiet in my throat.

I mourn a system in wonder,
a centre so florid, a battered
shield—and its soundless sunder
of itself, an autophagous matter,

cracked walnut under my chin,
ruined, base of my wings.

Hypos Envy a Hyper

A pair of stilts sashaying, she stole the waiting room
from the overweight women, their arms spilling white
fish bellies over the armchairs. She flits, a balloon string;
so thin, she irritates like a tube of fluorescent light.

Lips like ribbons, ribs like cheekbones, clavicles like aces,
pointed nails stretch her fingers into prongs—
what beauty, the patients seem to envy emaciation,
not knowing her sleepless hunger. Outside, throngs

with healthy bodies also like the look of bones.
But in here, she sits blushing, having noticed
being noticed. Why we stare at extremes—
we are not merely hangers for our habits,

if yellow fat tickles our sides,
if hunger bulges our eyes.

Harmony Lessons

for Ciaran Carson at 60

After the instruments lie fallow
for days or more, like harmless growth
gone to seed, come to flower,
they surprise with forgotten oaths.

Across continents, two notes seek a third,
as melody roots and harmonies ramble in.
In an interval of places, wood convoys hurt;
in Liverpool, slaves remain in the marble.
I expect hands came to mouths in America—
that notes opened into chords, and flute fingers
folded into hands to hold harmonicas—
to mull all the losses, to linger reels into the blue.

As you lead the time, I accord with my lungs,
harmonize as they rise, fingers to tongues.

Harmonica Lesson I

Bend the naturals; the notes aren't yours.
They're a fast fellowship of dusty lamps
waiting to be repaired in a cellar corner.
Bend every blow, snake them round the major,
match the note inside you. Through a capped well's
cracks, spit and whistle, set darkness to listen
to its depth. No one teaches you how to fill
a source, how to suck silver from the wind.

So play where no one hears you. In an orchard
stay to watch fruit fall, lie where crickets buzz.
Walk down long hills into loneliness where hard
men died. Squat where trains clack loose rails.

Play at the break of keys, sit on hollow stumps,
drift near dog kennels just to hear them howl.

Harmonica Lesson II

Sound undoes every layered name—
follow it out the window frame.
Go on, rise up, beneath the chord,
overcome and inhale slow, then hard.
Every strand winds into a melody,
notes blown like apple flowers off trees.
They bloom on hidden stems, and harmonies land
as cupped berries, spilling from your hands.

Harp songs lead into fields, unplowed,
open and aching, as silent lovers nod,
lift in the wind, settle as nestles, flutter
fingertips into kisses.
                        All you long for
comes into tune as you breathe sound.
Music grows from upturned ground.

Home Away

Family Country

Whose mother never said goodbye?
That was all left deep in the ocean,
in the sea air as they slumped beside
the railings? Goodbye, good riddance,
they said to the land, leaving bald hills
for pocket green, no baggage carried—
no new metaphors needed, no frills:
loss is the seed of hunger.

Those rugged hills, once meant, for me,
fullness—as we ate in a rain shower,
atop family country. How could they
have left this mountain, this sky over
a granite legend, high above Adrigole—
what never wavers, this Hungry Hill?

Hitching Tuam Road

for Seamus Heaney

I found a rhythm of walking today
on a rare Illinois road in Ireland,
hefting my pack between lifts
on a thirty-mile stretch till Tuam.

Beneath a crow teetering on a line
I stopped and on my thumb
balanced the wavering road, splitting
the oncoming from the passed.

The sun came to *Maigh Eo* today
dancing on car roofs, flecking the blue.
I turned my year tracing those gleams
into constellations, known and new.

I marked the year as the land,
one sun hitching open expanse.

(Co. Mayo, August 5th, 1995)

29th Birthday
(Co. Kerry, August 5th, 1997)

for my mother and hers

I. Skitching

False starts, stalled parts, near the edge of turning
over, my host's car engine wouldn't catch.
We dried the plugs, popped the clutch,
gave it a jump to surge the juice,
but in the end called Cronin up
to tow it down Killaha.

"Remember now to keep your line taut
particularly when you go downhill,"
said Cronin the younger, gesturing
on how to pump the brakes gently
to keep the nylon rope tight.
But only doing cinched the lesson.

Now if uphill towing was like follow-the-leader,
downhill rolling was like crack-the-whip.
I tapped the pedal every few moments
to avoid the jerk from a slack line:
a broken cord would have set me loose,
coasting off on my own.

And once when I rode the brakes, so not to tailgate,
the wheels locked—the catenary snapped
taut, and the mini skitched wide
in an arc with centrifugal speed—
I froze like a boy bumper-skiing,
skimming ice, gripping a cold cord.

41

I felt my year turn in that instant,
barrelling down the mountain in a worn-out car—
hauled through turns I'd known only by cycling and sauntering.
In the speed, I glimpsed only one familiar sight:
the frightened pair of eyes flashing
back in the rear-view.

II. Cords

Arriving in Kenmare, grease under my nails,
over soup and brown bread in the Horseshoe pub,
Dennis, bass-player and publican, leans over:
"There's the man who just succeeded Bruton,
Bertie, the leader of our country, just there,
not trailed by guards, cameras, or crowds,
just lunching with the wife and daughter."
With six elbows and flowers on the table,
the politician on holiday sits like any old man:
aloof, stupefied, buttering his bread.

No one minds him-with-the-reins-of-Éire-
in-his-hands. Everyone seems occupied
by their own affairs, upsets, goings-on,
their own slippery lives. We all track
our bloodless revolutions every year,
ticking off days of local bothers,
family squabbles, money troubles,
rarely marking a day of witness.
But today, I make myself that present,
to watch the photo-ready family having tea.

I think, I could join them, that first family of lies,
and be the silent son to the silent father,
to the Taoiseach, just through tea-time,
just till the minder said the car was ready. Perhaps,
they need a quiet brother for the silent sister,
a dumb son for the dumb mother.
We could explore our anamnesis during the lulls—
one to reconnoiter on this day
when my cord was cut
and I was spanked into breath.

But I stay on my stool, chewing bread,
aching in thought. I decide I'll stay
        wherever I go today,
take my boots off the roads,
unlace my mind from my lessons,
        go back to trace my living
        in the contours of my day.

III. Walnuts

In Illinois whenever my family built a bonfire, after we tossed
the brush, limbs, leaves, logs, branches, briar bundles, mown
grass, dead clippings, garden weeds, stiff feral, flattened
pumpkins, apple-orchard prunings, rotten boards,
railroad ties, broken chairs, and wooden rubbish
onto the heap, I'd gather up in my newspaper-
delivery satchel a horde of lemony
walnut fruit & drop them
one by one
into the burning pile.

I longed then to hear of mysteries—to learn
of tribal wrongs that could sear me;
to know how whites set upon the Sangamon,
and how the river flowed before;
to resurrect the Illini and hear
stories of the fields that lashed out
from piles of flaming light;
to hear what walnuts roasted in dying
embers could cure or curse; to know
why this flatland was one way

and not another.
But we are from places we do not know.

IV. Borders

As I walked up Main Street to Cronin's
to see about the mini, I stopped by a stone
wall near the park where once I kissed
a German woman I barely knew.

A man I'd played in a band with
came up and gave me a thump.
It had been years since we'd last sung
Moondance on a wet night at Murty's.

But we caught up in a moment, and he asked
what was off in the park. I told him I was,
once, kissing Antje on the shore under oak limbs—
how the tide sneaked in over our shoes.

He laughed and told me about being a boy
in Dublin and kissing behind the walls,
out of the street lights, away
from windows on summer nights.

Walls and fences, we concluded,
allow as much as they disallow.
We began to recall, as if for scrutiny,
those walls and fences we knew by touch.

He recalled Dublin stone and London iron
and ended with Berlin cement, crumbling down.
I told him of the wooden slat fences
I walked atop as a boy, and of the barbed-wire

museum in DeKalb Illinois,
of razor-wire coils that slinky
around garden fences in Greenwich Village,
and of the high granite walls that keep

Newport's rich off the streets.
I thought then to ask him if he's seen
the new wire fences in these mountains
and their wooden posts—

stakes of pine driven into rocky soil,
stakes that sprout down, draw water up,
shoot sprigs into air and live again—
he said: it is a wonder and someday,

maybe forests will again blanket Ireland.
We stood quiet, he seeing the new woods,
me wondering at the fences in my memory,
the borders that reveal the places I've known,

the places I've lived, the boundaries I've walked,
the ones I've crossed, the ones I've stopped at,
the borders that kept me from knowing the place
I am. What stays in me is what keeps me out.

Before we part, he asks, "Just where is it,
then, you come from Joe? Boston, is it?"
        I never know how to answer that.
Sometimes, I play the Yank, the farm-boy,

the Brooklyn tough, or the Irish-come-
home-again, never knowing a simple assent.
But today, I know to smirk, "I come from
my mother; today is my birthday."

V. Tale Told

After learning the mini could not be fixed for days,
I found myself heading to the Lansdowne Hotel
for a pint, where an old man—looking like
he'd sat there all day—directed my attention
to the wall: a poster for a rock band
announced in magic marker they will play
here, Friday the 8th: "Be There!"
He asks if I see something strange in that.

"No, not really," I answer—does he?
"Be There" he intones, reading the poster,
"Isn't that queer?" he asks,
"Why did they not write, 'Be Then'?

Answer that one, Yank, true,
you'll know as much as I do."

VI. Neidín

In the time I have left, I'll thumb over my bildungsromance—
when I backed away from America, stepped out with chance,

came to meet a man I barely knew, to climb, to write, to read,
to love, to watch as he drew on walls and griped about Irish greed.

I met cousins in Bantry, spent nights in Kenmare, or Neidín,
"little nest" (of thieves—as the English used to claim).

I mined meaning from names, traced lines of fault
swivelling through time, but found no source, no result,

outside tenancy and power. To see where we are, look behind;
to know where to go, trace the contours of our minds.

VII. Obair chloiche

On my return, the old boys welcomed me home from the corner,
nodding as I walked toward the stone circle in the old town centre—

granite hunks inlaid in dirt (the cobbles came later)—
I heard about the lever-works of its makers;

how they dug and heaved to plant hewn stone in fosses;
silent stories in rocky soil, circling patterns of losses.

Townlands forget their names as progress loosens
tongues from history, as a dead Blasket woman summons

dreamers to dreams, warning with whispers: "Without words,
we have no memories. Listen for what is never heard."

VIII. Bothar na gCapall

My cousin Sean, Adrigole's postman, is making a name list—
of hills, roads, and fields, of names the cartographers missed:

Bothar na gCapall, a pass on a road where hooves no longer clatter.
Only for *seanduine* and postmen does the name still echo matter.

But the hoof beats still resound somewhere. Sound waves
without a final shore, outlast us, diminish only over space.

Walls in Famine villages, once washed by families long dead,
still sweat starvation. The shepherd's beds,

stone huts, are not sealed off—the mossy smoke holes
send up ferns, green columns, rooting in dead coals.

Appassionata

for Alexander Gargilis

Neighbours see we're not yet leaving:
two strangers settling Killaha,
my sweater nightly unweaving
under cracking ceiling stars.
Looking up in bed, I lie
as Alex addles Beethoven,
and moonlight beads the gladioli,
trimmed for a Kerry coven.

Yellow furze braces the fuchsia
encircling *Dracena* inside the fences.
Painting poems beneath chalk vistas,
we damn to hell simple sequences,
upbraid consequences. We swim nude
in mountain pools that pull down legs;
we peel and eat whole kiwi fruit,
drink our tea to the dregs.

At night from the grand piano
before the glowing electric coals,
Alex trills Chopin's moody tones,
appealing for the night to be whole.
From his fingers old romances escape;
in flourishes of minor keys,
a half-century of lovers traipse
his fingers, rain off the eaves.

If Vermeer Were Here

for Eamon Grennan

    he might chart her shoulder
onto this corridor of road
and journey-work of grass.
Her sloping neckline shares
    the bus window; it holds her
head up to ranging clouds,
as green steel overpasses
shadow wave her hair.

    A bright candescence sails
her off cherry-blue traffic
as cars paste loose leaves
to air and rusty stone,
    to wending cobalt rails.
She sleeps in her jacket,
yellow crackling her sleeves
static rustles her backbone.

    Traced strokes might capture
the weight of her jostling
breast and her airy
hands, fingers unfurled.
    But how could he venture
to paint this eye opening,
this fast involuntary
defiance of the world?

Moose

still for Joanne

Untangling a tired argument,
we scanned for pilot whales
off Cape Breton's cliffs, trying
to make out Prince Edward Island.
Below us, two eagles spiralled high
above the water by the rock face.
Watching them, you calmed
while I made light of our fight,
comparing us to the raptors
circling a bare nest.

We stayed to see the sun
set over water, still on tenterhooks,
then pulled into the fir trees' night.
I rushed ahead fooling, feigning
a poor ambush.
                     But I kept in sight.
Near the trail head, you shushed me
as I ran laughing, then urged me
in a spat whisper to stop.
When I turned, you were frozen,
except your hands fluttered low.

The bull moose grazed in a clearing.
I'd run right past him, but you traced
the bushes and grasses waving in his wake
to watch him revolve to regard you.
Blindly my hand went to yours,
and, bumping, we found our clasp.
His stature dazed us—
                     his shoulder hump,
seven-feet high; his coat the sheen
of smooth bark in rain; his great head
streaming a gulf of beard. As he

rose I met his black eyes and fell
lost into still sight, his eye drawing
mine like a luminous detail of paint
seizes a scene.
                    He betrayed no curiosity,
no surprise, no fear, only the alert
patience of an oaken animal.
Standing there, I felt sudden,
less like a sinuous interloper,
staring at him, slack-jawed,
like a moon-faced monkey.

For a full minute, nothing stirred,
only a twig dangling in his rack—then neck
muscles rippled and a hoof raised; he stomped
twice, snorting, but stopped at your whisper:
"You're not staring at him—are you?"
I turned to see you:
                    head lowered,
shoulders bent, eyes averted, surveying
indirectly—you knew to how to observe
askance, like watching the sun
eclipse through a pin hole.

Nothing in nature is as naked
as a human face. Only an owl's
high-ruff collar and feather jowls
rival our stare in flat intimidation.
Our frontal gazes shout—*charge or cede*—
even when they mean to fathom.
We crept to the car, but I returned
still struck with a camera—just
caught his outline, breaching the trail,
backlit and whole, defined by shadow.

Act IV

Anger swims with anger. I raise my voice
with you; my father hovers in my words.
Everything said fades like distant noise
to the stark fact: I killed the birds

nesting in the airshaft. You wonder
how could I do it, a cleaning so cruel.
The pigeon chicks chirped under eaves,
and I, a magpie in another's roost,
pushed, for sanitation, the whole life down,

ledge to cement, home and eggs.
Amid the garbage, a chick on the ground,
no life, a metaphor on dead legs.

But sadism does not lodge in me,
pain just coloured me wickedly.

Making Change

How fast she counts, her long aqua nails
flashing over the till. A wonder
she doesn't break them more often.

My turn, I take my full, red-leather
coin purse. A small pleasure
to hand her the precise amount,

exact change being the best kind.
If only it was as easy to keep open
the purse, pursed inside.

I want to handle possibility,
slide out, sift change from worn
repetitions, exchanges.

When I count coins, I sluice nickels,
dimes, quarters, pennies into my palm,
tabulate as I pick them,

fast double-check the sum,
place or push them over the counter.
Making change, I know,

isn't just about counting,
it's about trusting what adds up
is in your hands.

Cleaning the Pool

for my brother Stephen

Before you or others rose, I stirred
the brocade of leaves, fallen petals
and seeds that floated in the pool.
Hatched lattices of yellow light

in the robin-shell pool after the storm.
You, just back from Pakistan's
tribal areas, distinguish here
and there, but I don't know enough.

I skim with a long pole, draw
a mouth of clotted leaves in the net.
I wonder how the water runs through mountains
in regions where empires have killed decades,

militaries unraveled in stone, where dust
barters tanks, what irrigation schemes can change.

A rug you carried home—red, black, and blue thread,
woven into bombs, bullets, tanks, grenades—

was patiently dyed, Afghan wool looped
into icons, now in our parents' home.
Your son and wife miss you
when you fly to foreign homelands.

Sleep, hunker this morning;
I'll skim from the pool
take what has fallen,
and mound it by the stairs.

Last night we argued about rewriting
the past. This morning is
numinous, blue, white, no
swimmers touching bottom.

"Blue Eye"

for us three

pulls hundreds of underworld miles
here into unwinding peace aquatic:
a spring of sight—*po, po*—a mesmeric eye.
Albanian water tumbles to the Adriatic
from a source under sienna mountains,
a cataract ringed by blinking mosses.
Alive in childhood memories Steve flies
from a clay ridge into rising liquid roses,
a bone-skin plunge of nerve and ice.
Jim steps over smooth stones, rinsing
his ankles, wades into the cold freshet,
then dives under watermelons bobbing.
I fall to revive, quench thirst, fear, heat—
into the lens where brothers meet.

(Near Delvinë, Albania)

Whose Woods

In memory, Mary Mitchell Lennon (1918-2005)

We read the poet Frost aloud as you, Gram,
unwound your days. You could not see to see
us cousins, brothers, sisters, children, friends
gather as new growth—deep-tangled wild, green—
climbed your stone walls. Whose woods these are,
we think you know—the woods, dark, full of sleep.
Poems read by the respirator, as way turned onto way,
you parted yourself—like leaves in the brook that leapt
around your life, your gardens blooming and fading.
As I read, "I doubted if I should ever come back,"
your squeeze sent a gallop up under my ribs;
those words became rare flowers, took a new path:
you've overwritten Frost, overtaken Emily;
you leaned out the window and left the family.

Home Body Home

for Susan

We can learn from a tree about ecstasy,
watching it writhe or whip in the wind.
Oaks and elms out the window, elementary,
show us how deep we can bend.

Diagnosis seems like a promise:
life will change, begin again a plan.
But across thresholds of premises,
hope swings and closes to the jambs.

Still, we knock on oak doors and linger,
tap lightly for rot, for veneers, and mind
panes painted shut, then slide fingers
into wall cracks to let in air at thirty-nine.

Just so, a body opens, unrehearsed—
when you listen to hurts, hinges burst.

Street Corner in Mumbai

I. Goods Carrier

Krishna painted on a goods carrier in Mumbai
surveys over hot engines; a fiery eagle
spans the radiator grill, triangles play,
blue and white, orange and red,
in patterns down the metal lace.

Bright blue like spring water, Krishna's
face is the apex of a pyramid framing
the white clouds in the tinted windshield,
the unseen driver's braceleted elbow
folding, unfolding out of the window.

Krishna's mien is not otherworldly, not
joyous but even-handed, straight-lipped,
almost midwestern; his eyes lowered
to where rickshaws swerve past
with horn blasts and soot fumes.

His aura is of clear sky, oranges, and milk.
Black locks fall round his face; gold hoops
dangle above the cobra wreathing his neck.
He, the Chance of chances,
I hear, is one with his image.

II. Mudflaps and Bumpers

On the newly paved road, in forest greens, holy orange,
god blue, and man gold, the truck parades with Krishna's blessing.
As it passes, the driver blows the horn and waves to a skinny boy
leaping on a side street. How familiar. To get horn blares as kids,
we pulled at cords in air at eighteen wheelers passing,

Yosemite Sam or Playboy bunnies on their mudflaps.
Here, a grim-tusked, yellow-horned, red-eyed,
moustached demon head rides the painted bumper, floating
bodiless above "DANGER" in blood-red English,
warning passers of unforeseeable turns.

III. Side-Street Story

On the unpaved side street, a boy in a dishrag shirt
walks barefoot toward me carrying a long bendy stick.
A thin-plumed crow lands down in front of him, zeroed
in on the oily body of a rat nestled in the gutter refuse.

The bird pokes, pecks, flips the greasy body with its black beak,
tosses the loose-skinned, worm-tailed meat to the street.
Swift wings untuck, arc after the still rat. Tossing it again,
the crow could eat in a moment; blood would dowse the fur.

As a claw tenders the body, the boy charges by the barbers
and customers in the geometry of summer's shade,
tilts his lance at the hunter, shouting,
swearing in blue passion at the crow.

The crow skulks as Kali or the Morrigán,
then takes to the air over the boy's mad branch.

He swings and wheels—a banyan in a monsoon fable—
under the dark fingers that fly off and fold on a cable.

The men turn away; the boy drops his lance, squats.
He waves his fingers over the six-inch body,
in a hungry show of death rites, or a shadow dance
to wake a sleeper? The greasy rat flips, oddly

alert in the hot world, its opossum show over.
Bent-whiskered on rubber haunches, it sniffs,
scampers away from the boy who hovers
as it scuttles, its black eyes bobbling, it slips

toward its drain gate. No one sees the crow leap—
but the boy sees the cable sway then leaps, waves,
which the driver of a passing goods carrier sees, blares
his horn, scares the crow. By chance, a rat saved.

Santa Maria del Boschetto

for Mariella and Marika, Mary and Donna Marie

Beside the Church of the Virgin, rows of ex voto
paintings hang in the cortile. Each shows when
the Mother shared grace, saved with a look
children in danger, sailors at sea, sickened men,

the many vivid souls in peril. The corners seem
rubbed away to reveal the glorious light, Herself,
burnished babe in arms, glowing like coals through
a bedroom ceiling, steaming open grey clouds.

She beams grace to sailors pleading on deck,
fastened to toppled masts with death gazes
in waves as storms atomize the perspective.
She radiates hope in a watercoloured haze,

as a sunspot over a dizzy banister—a mild
minister of grace to a prone child

mirrored in a red pool of his life—
for thin fishermen with cannibal eyes.

Always, some soul prayed for her to appear.
Over the scene of disaster she surveys with chary
eyes, the same look in dollar votive candles
in West Harlem, our Technicolor Mary.

Survivors enskyed Her above the scenes,
so viewers could see the moment of rescue, see
Her burst the blue with gold as a child plummets
headlong from a sheer window of Camogli.

How that kid lived—such falls make ghosts—
we do not see. But above horror there is succour,
and for families hurt and whole on the Ligurian coast:
grace in the homes of the wives by the sea.

(Camogli, Italy)

Above Rapallo in the Sun

for our son Nicholas

"This is for the birds," you say, strewing
strands of your chestnut hair into the *maestro*.
You hold your red comb, without irony
in your voice, and pull hairs that will glow

as filaments when your fingers wave
them over the walk in the wind.

What doesn't matter, here above
Rapallo in the sun, safe with friends,
is how you might mean two things
but do not. What matters is the nonchalant
hope you seem to have, wondering

whether your strands might soften
some swallow's nest, alongside
some mother's feathers.

(10 Agosto, 2007)

Coda

Bethesda

Strolling up the mall in Central Park
the angel appears, the one in Kushner's
trilogy. Her face is just at eye mark,
but at the balcony, standing closer,
I see how high she rises above her ground.

The lengths many of us go just to hover
at a common height—really, what bounds
even to rise from under the covers.

Often to soar means only to get
to the eye level of others—but if two feet
off the earth feels like leaving the planet,
why peg it only a little leap?

Even small ascensions
beat waiting for heaven.

Coeliac disease is an auto-immune disorder that damages the small intestine and interferes with the absorption of food. The only treatment is to avoid eating gluten, found in wheat, barley, triticale, rye, as well as gluten-contaminated foods. The disease has often gone undiagnosed, especially in the United States, where its malnutrition and fatigue affect roughly one in one-hundred-and-thirty people. The symptoms of the untreated disease are a nagging hunger, cramps, weight loss, exhaustion, bloating, loose stools, bone and joint pain, and low blood pressure. Its secondary illnesses include ulcers, anaemia, hypothyroidism, hyposplenism, osteoporosis, dermatitis herpetiformis, infertility, and liver damage. This is a treatable disease.

About the Author

JOSEPH LENNON was born in Newport, Rhode Island, and grew up in Rochester, a small town in central Illinois. He has lived in Ireland and Italy and travelled throughout India. After a decade in New York City, teaching at Manhattan College, he now lives in Philadelphia with his family and is Director of Irish Studies at

Villanova University. He has published poetry and critical essays on Irish literature and postcolonial studies. His book *Irish Orientalism: A Literary and Intellectual History* (Syracuse UP, 2004) won the Donald J. Murphy Prize for Distinguished First Book from the American Conference for Irish Studies. Lennon spent many years living with undiagnosed coeliac disease and its effects.